A Visionary's Guide: Sell Your Home for Top Dollar

How to choose a Realtor who's looking out for you, not out to get you!

Gary Krieger

ISBN 978-1-4303-0474-6

Printed in the United States of America.
Realtor® is a registered trademark of the National
Association of Realtors.
Cover Photo by
Michael McCreary/Haven Studio
Construction by E.Y.U., Inc., dba California
Construction, 310-293-0646

Contents

My wife, Kim, my partner since we were young, my friend and the phenomenal mother of our children is one of the people who has blessed my life. With her support, dedication and love, I have been able to accomplish much. This book is dedicated to Kim, with love and gratitude.

Acknowledgements

I'd like to offer a special thanks to my family for their encouragement and support for this project, and for all the other endeavors I have ever undertaken. I have learned much from those closest to me including love, compassion, empathy, spirituality, kindness, negotiation and business. My wife, and my three amazing children, Matthew, Jeremiah and Sarah have been a great inspiration, and I thank them for all the lessons, both easy and difficult, that they have taught me! And, I thank my mother-in-law, Aurora, for editing this book. I love you all.

Thanks also to those people who have influenced my love of real estate and my decision to pursue my passion for real estate as a career. Many friends lent their support and ideas to my project, and I thank them all. Our office is full of supportive and dedicated professionals who have given freely of themselves and their knowledge to work as a team.

I'd like to give a special thanks to Lynne Weiss, who was our realtor, and who became our friend, my mentor and finally my colleague. She

i

was always available to teach, to coach and to help me learn the fine points of the Real Estate business from the broker's side of the table.

Forward

Positive energy attracts positive results. In selling one's home, the same law of the universe applies. I believe in the theory of attraction. The energy we send out attracts the energy we get back from the universe. In order to maximize your profits from the sale of your home, it helps if you believe, as I do, that the universe will provide the right buyer, at the right time, at the right price. You will see, it will happen.

This book is about maximizing the profits you realize from the sale of your home and the real estate process I use to make that happen for you. But it is more than that too. It is about your mindset and the approach you take to achieve your goals. There are many things you need to consider during the time you are thinking about selling your home. Once you've decided to sell, you will need to decide what's to be done before you put your home on the market and how those results will manifest themselves. Decisions you make during the critical time from thinking about selling to putting the home on the market can mean the difference of tens of thousands of dollars, even hundreds of thousands in multi-million dollar properties. Decisions made well can bring you huge returns and poor decisions can cost your dearly. So too, can positive or negative energy affect the outcome of the profit you receive.

Most people do not sell their home often. So, the process can be confusing and difficult. Real estate contracts were a simple 1 page document 30 years ago. Today, the contracts are like a small book. In the past, the byword was "caveat emptor", buyer beware. Today, full disclosure is imperative. Your failure to disclose any problems with your home can leave you vulnerable to massive litigation. The amount of paperwork is daunting, and continually changing. Each time a new lawsuit involving real estate is filed, it can lead to a new revision to the sales contracts, addenda or disclosure documents

One needs to be very careful to get all the details right so that a sale does not come back to haunt you and cost you untold misery dealing with the legal system, enormous legal expenses, and the possibility of large money judgments against you.

However, what we believe is what we receive. So think positively, expect that you will do everything correctly, follow the rules and the laws, take counsel from competent advisors, and all should end well for you.

This book is intended to provide general

information, and is not intended to provide legal or accounting advice. I am neither an attorney nor an accountant. Should you have any questions of a legal nature, contact your attorney. And likewise, contact your certified public accountant for accounting advice.

I will attempt to guide you through the steps you need to consider, the decisions you will need to make and the people who can help you with the process. You will learn about choosing a realtor and whether to use a large or small real estate company. The book will guide you in your choice of a full service real estate agent or a limited service, discount agent, the difference it can make to you and the amount of money you end up receiving from the sale. You will learn that little details can make a big difference and that there are mistakes to avoid.

My book deals with finding a real estate agent with integrity, passion and the desire to help you achieve your goals. It's about negotiating to get you the most money. It is about finding a real estate agent who puts your interests above his own. The book is written for you, the consumer, and is intended to provide you with information so that you can make the best, and most informed, decisions in your own best interest.

After reading the book, you will have a reference and a reference point for understanding the process. It will help you understand the process, the psychology and the effects of the market and the role your realtor plays.

As a full service agent with the largest global real estate firm, I have a distinct bias. I spoke with other real estate companies before I chose to affiliate with my company, and for the many reasons that I speak to in this book, I feel we offer the greatest benefit to my clients. I've tried to temper some of my bias with useful and helpful information to assist you in making your decisions.

For the purpose of simplicity and ease of reading, I will use only the masculine pronoun. However, in no way do I mean to imply that female realtors are not equal to male realtors. In my belief system, they are equal in every way.

Chapter 1:

<u>The Decision to Sell Your Home</u>

Getting started is sometimes the hardest part. As a rule, one doesn't awaken one morning and suddenly call a realtor to list one's home for sale. First, one begins to think about moving. As time progresses, people start to verbalize their thoughts and then the discussion amongst the owners begins.

Why do people choose to sell? The obvious answer is there are as many reasons as there are people. There are some general categories though which can be described and that will cover a broad range of situations. The subtext here is Motivation.

Motivation is the part of our psyche that arouses us to take action toward a desired goal. It is the reason for the action, and it is what gives us purpose and direction to behave as we do. Let's examine a number of common reasons people are motivated to sell their home.

Not necessarily in order or in order of importance, the first and perhaps the most obvious reason to sell your home is the desire to move to a larger home. In the past, we often purchased a home and remained there for life. In today's mobile society, we tend to move more often, even within the same geographic area.

First time home buyers eventually become first time home sellers. Since the hardest part of home ownership is getting into one's first home, it is often a home that is imperfect. Compromises are usually made when buying a first home and one may choose to sell it for a multitude of reasons.

It's not uncommon for a first home to be in a location which wasn't ideal. It may be too small. Features may be all wrong and the overall "package" can be impractical. Or, everything can be lovely, but you may need a larger home. One may quickly outgrow a first home.

The good news is a first home gave you the opportunity to gain equity while living there. It certainly makes the purchase of the next home easier and provides capital for stepping up to a home that meets more of your requirements. With each move, and each subsequent move, we seem to get closer to the home that really works for us. Of course, those requirements may continue to change over time.

Moving up is common due to family changes. More children mean the need for more bedrooms and more bathrooms. Older children usually need a larger yard. Maybe a pool has become a new requirement.

Once a hill dweller, family circumstances change and may dictate a flat yard with plenty of play room and sidewalks for bikes and skateboard riding. Hill property can be very impractical for families with young children. Can you imagine how frustrating it is when a ball rolls downhill and it keeps on rolling for blocks!

Of course the opposite can also apply. As young children grow up, parents may then be able to move to a home that may have been impractical just a few years earlier. So, one may move into the hills from flat ground.

School districts vary and many people move to get their children into a better school. Or, a move may be to get closer to work. After all, a long commute is inconsistent with adequate family time.

Taste changes and people often want to move to a different style home. Not uncommonly, as we grow older, we like things we once didn't like and want change to reflect our new style. Since there are so many architectural styles, there is a veritable smorgasbord of choices from which to pick.

Inheritance and job promotion may add capital or income to increase one's ability to afford a more expensive home. The ability to buy up is a powerful motivator for many. Life cycle events account for a large percent of homeowners choosing to move.

Life changes can create a need to sell a home. Divorce may necessitate the sale of the family home. And, of course there may be a great deal of emotion involved when a sale is forced by the break up of a marriage. The death of one spouse results in another significant life change. A widow or widower may not want to stay in a home after the death of a loved one. The memories may just be too painful, or the financial circumstances may dictate the need to sell. In any event, death and divorce account for many, many sales.

A job transfer creates another significant reason for moving. For those facing a corporate relocation, certain special circumstances come into play.   While there are many problems and opportunities created by a job transfer, many of the usual issues surrounding the sale of a property can be mitigated by Corporate Relocation Departments.

Generally, and briefly, a Corporate Relocation Department is affiliated with a network of high quality realtors, moving specialists, and logistics managers to help make the process as easy as possible. Most often, a home under contract with a relocation department is "sold" at a pre-determined price, after a pre-determined time on the market, whether or not an immediate buyer is found. That is, the Relocation Department or

The Decision to Sell Your Home

Company purchases the home and continues to market it. Therefore, the seller becomes free to move and purchase a new home in the new job location. If you are involved with a Corporate Relocation Company, you will undoubtedly receive a full package of information that will keep you reading for hours!

We spend a lifetime moving up to bigger and better homes. We move from area to area, school district to school district, city to city. We move to fulfill status needs and we move to be closer to relatives. Reasons for these decisions seem infinite.

After a lifetime of moving up, our children grow up and move out. Suddenly, we're living in very large home, and rattling around in all the empty space. What was once a place filled with activity and love has become an empty shell. So, the "empty nesters" may decide to move to be closer to their children, or grandchildren.

Or, perhaps the owners just want to cash out equity. Maybe they want to move down to a more manageable sized home and bank the cash remainder. The liquidation of equity in one's home, built up over a lifetime, assists in one's retirement. Since a home is often the largest personal asset one has, it becomes a viable funding source for augmenting retirement.

Another reason homes are sold fall into the investment category. Equity build up may dictate a tax deferred exchange, IRS Section 1031, to transfer equity to a more productive investment. So, sale of investment homes and small apartment units, duplexes, triplexes and four-plexes, constitute another source of sale. While the same amount of emotion may not be involved in the sale of investment property as in the sale of a primary residence, a similar process of decision making is involved.   In fact, it may be more important to focus on the issues surrounding a tax deferred exchange because of the complexity of the IRS code. You should always consult your CPA and your attorney when you are dealing with a tax deferred exchange. You will also need the services of a company to mediate the exchange, known as an accommodator. Strict guidelines apply to 1031 exchanges, and a misstep along the way may disqualify you from the tax deferred status you are trying to achieve.   So, proceed cautiously and deliberately to protect your interests.

No doubt, this is merely a summary of a few of the reasons why people choose to sell property. Your personal situation and events in your life may dictate countless other reasons, all of which are valid and just as compelling.

All the above, and so many more reasons I haven't discussed, provide the motivation for selling one's home.   So why worry about motivation?   Why does your realtor care about motivation?   Why should buyers care about the motivation? Understanding answers to these questions about your motivation will help clarify the process and thus simplify the decisions that will need to be made along the way.

First and foremost, you want to be clear as to why you want to sell. In this instance, you are the most important people, and if you're not absolutely clear about your motives, then the decision to sell becomes laden with conflict. Since there is often a lot of emotional charge that accompanies the sale of one's home, a clear understanding begins to bridge the process. For your own mental health, it is best to have completed this process so that you are in control of the difficult decisions you'll need to make.

Your realtor wants to know why you want to sell. By understanding your motivation, he can suggest options for best meeting your goals. Strategies for pricing and marketing may be tailored specifically to help you achieve the desired result. For instance, an elderly couple moving to a retirement community may prefer to take more of the proceeds of the sale as income and thus they may want to offer primary or secondary financing to a buyer. This can create a win-win situation for both the buyer and seller. However, if the seller's broker doesn't know that the seller is motivated to generate income, then he can't serve their best interests.

You want to have a realtor who understands

your motivation and asks you pertinent questions about your motivation. The more your Realtor comprehends your motives, the better he is able to help you achieve your desired outcome. Sometimes, it takes a lot of questioning and probing and following up to ascertain the real motivation, but once it is clear, options often become available to better serve you and help you with your sales strategy.

Buyers and buyers' brokers want to know what motivates the sellers. They sometimes use the information to help structure deals, and sometimes may want to use the knowledge to take advantage of a situation. It behooves you to choose your realtor carefully so that he doesn't become an unwitting ally of the buyer. I'll talk more about choosing a realtor, ethics and due diligence when I get to that chapter. For now, suffice to say that this is an extremely important aspect of your decision.

Now that we know what motivates the seller, we need to identify the target market. Who are the most likely people to purchase your property? How do we best reach them? These are important questions on which your realtor needs to focus. Once the target audience is defined, some of the questions about how to present your home to the marketplace will automatically be defined. You and your realtor can discuss these issues and agree on a course of action.

Chapter 2:

<u>Pre-Sale Preparations</u>

The philosophy of getting your home ready to market can be divided into a number of categories. The questions to ask relate back to goals and motivation. Certain improvements can have a relatively large payback and maximal impact for a limited investment, and may be the best improvements to make prior to marketing a property. Other investments in repairing and upgrading your home may not return all the investment you've made, and thus may be a poor choice. Any improvements made must be viewed from the eyes of potential buyers. This is not true of improvements you make to your home when you are planning to stay in your home. Of course, then, you do what pleases you and what you wish to live with for the duration. However, it is always a better investment if you couple your desires with a long term goal of selling, keeping in mind what a buyer eventually will think of what you've done.

Some sellers choose not to do anything to their home before putting it on the market. That decision is just as valid as choosing to make repairs and improvements. Sometimes a seller prefers to discount the value of the work needed to be done rather than do it himself. Of course there are always consequences to all our decisions and in this case, the seller is likely to take a hit on the price of his home.

Before you do anything else, de-clutter your home. Generally, the fewer belongings you have, the better. Put away all the extra things you love that detract from a buyer looking at your home. You are selling your home, not your furnishings and decorations. You want buyers to focus on the property and imagine their belongings in the house. The less of your furnishings that you have, the better they will be able to imagine their own possessions in the home.

The first, and possibly the most important aspect of the pre-sale preparation for marketing your home, is to look at the first impression your home will make. It always makes a statement, and the only question is what kind of a statement does it make? Hopefully, your home makes a positive statement, not a negative one. Let's explore how potential buyers view your home.

A buyer often looks at your home as a project in need of work and repair. Even if you have maintained your property, buyers are skeptical. After an agreement is reached and a potential sale is in the offing, escrow is opened. Buyers typically have 17 days after the agreement is accepted to do all of their inspections and remove their contingencies.

One of the ways to avoid surprises, and a valuable pre-sale tool, is for the seller to do the inspections before the property is put on the market. In that way, any problems will be known from the start, and you, the seller will be forearmed. Depending on the problems that are discovered, you can choose to ignore them and understand that a buyer will discount the property to repair them. I think a better choice, is to have the problems repaired. Use licensed contractors, pull permits when needed, and keep receipts. If you do the inspections and make the repairs, you have removed the uncertainty of purchasing your home and created opportunity for an easier sale.

Curb appeal is the first thing a buyer will notice. What impression does your home make as the buyer first drives up the street and sees your home? If your home has a great deal of curb appeal, people get excited. They want to get out of the car and are anxious to take a look. Remember, more often than not, this is a visceral and emotional response. There is an old adage that says, "You don't have a second chance to make a first impression". I can tell you from personal experience that when you drive up to a home that doesn't meet your aesthetic expectations, the buyer will often say, "I don't even want to go into that home", and will turn around and leave. It is NOT in your best interest as a seller to lose any potential buyer for a reason as simple as improving curb appeal.

My first recommendation to sellers interested in maximizing the sale proceeds of their home is to focus on improving curb appeal. The fix can be as easy as planting a few flats of annual color plants that are in bloom for the season. Flowers and bright blossoms go a long way toward making a house look like a home. Sometimes, a few well placed shrubs and a tree or two may also make a big difference. Of course, if your home already looks sensational, you may not need to do anything. But, in almost every home, more flowers can improve the look at very little expense. When you are in the planning stage, the sooner you add bedding plants, the better. Most of the annual color plants start out as small stems, with or without blossoms. They do grow rapidly though, so if you can get a few weeks head start on the growth cycle, you'll have more to show when your home is presented for sale.

Remember too, when you list your home for sale, your Realtor will begin to prepare marketing materials for your home. If you've just planted the annual color, it won't look as good in the photographs and on the brochures as it would when it's grown and filled in.

While I'm talking about the exterior, and particularly the garden, let's look at the overall state of the garden. Is it in character with the garden and home design? As an example, an English Cottage may have an overgrown look and feel which is utterly charming, quaint and inviting. However, with a different style home, that same garden may look cluttered, unkempt and, worst of all, may project a sense that this home is not well maintained. So, if trees need trimming, bushes need thinning, weeds need pulling and grass needs greening, do it! These are all fairly low cost solutions and add immeasurably to curb appeal and desirability.

Exterior painting is probably the next most cost effective improvement after landscaping. Take a look at your home. Is the paint fading and peeling? Does your home have a decent paint job, but with colors that are dated and out of favor? If the answer is yes, then consider painting your home with the current color palate that is attracting buyers in today's market. Just be sure that the colors you choose to paint are in the mainstream, popular and have design sophistication to them. Spruce up the exterior and you will almost certainly draw more buyers! Since finding the right buyer is a numbers game, the more potential buyers you can attract, the higher the likelihood of a quick sale.

A fresh coat of paint inside the home is also a good investment. Be careful here though. Don't fall into the trap of creating a "blank canvas" for the buyer by painting everything white. Many buyers are turned off by a "white-out". The home doesn't show nearly as well with the "everything white" theme. Again, as with the exterior, choosing colors that are being used in the current color palate in design homes can give you a guide.

Some homes have a bad odor that smacks you in the face when you walk in. Buyers are turned off by strong pet odors and heavily spiced food odors. The odors can drive away buyers who might otherwise have an interest in your home. The odors can have a detrimental effect on a price a buyer might offer. Make sure that your home doesn't smell bad, and if it does, take whatever steps are necessary to get rid of those bad odors.

Ideally, your home will have a fresh, clean smell. Buyers are attracted to emotional, visceral stimuli. Think about what your home smells like. Vanilla scented candles burning in the home elicit positive and strong responses from buyers. Freshly baked cookies, hot from the oven, also do that. There is definitely a subliminal response and I think the kid in each of us remembers back to happy memories of warm, freshly baked treats!

Another project that really freshens up a home is to replace worn knobs and handles.

Change faucet handles, door knobs and cabinet knobs. These items often show a lot of wear and tear, and new handles and knobs can make a big difference. Your hardware superstores can provide a large selection of all the items you need at a reasonable price. It is an investment well worth the little time and energy it takes. Either a handy homeowner or a handyman can do the job quickly.

Once you leave the realm of landscaping and paint and inexpensive decorating items, the decisions to spend money to improve your home get dicier. There's always a balance between what needs to be done, and what you think needs to be done! For example, if the carpeting is worn, stained, unraveling, stretched and generally not looking good, you may make a decision to replace, or remove the carpets. If you have hardwood floors under the carpets, it may be a good idea to simply remove the carpet and refinish the floors. If not, choose new carpeting, but again do so with the current design styles and colors in mind. Green shag carpet went out of fashion in the 70's, so a bargain on green shag would not be a good replacement choice (of course fashions change, and one day green shag carpet may be the rage again)!

There is one way to capitalize on the interior design trends and capture the currently selling ideas without spending any money, just some time. Visit the model showrooms of large developers who are building homes in your general area. Typically, the developers spend a great deal of money consulting with top designers. Their goal, as is yours, is to sell homes. Of course, their business is developing land, building homes and selling them. Their investment in their model homes can mean that you get the best ideas for your improvements free. Then, you get to sell your home for the maximum possible profit also.

There are different schools of thought about getting into the realm of major improvements. Some, like replacing a roof that has reached the end of its service life with a new roof, or replacing galvanized water pipes with copper pipes can improve the salability of a home, but not necessarily increase the value substantially. If you make these types of improvements, you eliminate the negative comments a buyer will see from a home inspection service.

When buyers get negative remarks from home inspectors, they automatically try to negotiate for the most money they might need to repair the problem. By doing the repair before the sale, you mitigate the issue. You control how much you spend to make the repair, and as long as you do a quality job, using a licensed contractor and obtaining building permits, you will probably save money in lieu of having the buyer do it.

Once you have done the inspections and made the repairs, your agent can use the reports as another marketing tool. They can be displayed in a notebook and offered to any interested, serious buyers for their review. The review, along with the repair records and receipts, will allay any fears that the buyer may have regarding the condition of your home. Your buyer may choose to have his own inspections done, but any conflict that may arise is then subject to review with your own inspector and argued by your inspector with their inspector. Many times, the buyers will simply accept the report of your inspector. It is important for your agent to recommend that you use a highly regarded inspector, as it will go a long way towards generating confidence that the report is accurate and reliable. Every obstacle that can be removed in the process of selling your home is a good thing, and a benefit to you.

Let's go back to the idea of doing major remodeling before you sell. What about remodeling a bathroom or a kitchen? If you have the budget to remodel, and you have the time to remodel, and you have the desire to remodel, then it may be well worth the investment. Provided, however, you do the project tastefully and with the current design trends in mind. Again, use the large developer's model homes as your design showroom and follow their design ideas. If you do that, you are probably going to profit from your investment.

That being said, think about the questions

about remodeling mentioned above. Do you have the budget to remodel? A kitchen remodel can cost tens of thousands of dollars depending on the choices you make. A bathroom can cost five thousand dollars and up. The first question to answer then is whether you have the funds, or want to borrow the money to do the remodel.

The second question to ask is whether you have the time to remodel. The question can be divided into two parts. First, do you personally have the time to do all the preparatory work, doing the research, meeting with a designer, choosing the "parts and pieces" and the myriad of other decisions required? It can be a time consuming and challenging task, unless you hire a professional to do all the work for you. Of course, that is an additional expense.

Secondly, your timetable for selling your home is important. A kitchen remodel can take up to several months, depending on how you approach the project. Are you willing to delay putting your home on the market until the project is completed? How does that impact your decision? Are you willing to delay your move until this can all be done, or are there other considerations about the move? Do you have enough time, for instance, to plan for the enrollment of your children in a new school district and still have time to do the remodel and find a new home? As you can see, there are many questions you need to answer that surround the decision and your timetable for selling.

Finally, do you have the stamina to remodel? This is really the most serious question. Remodeling takes a certain personality, and you need to decide whether you can handle all that goes along with remodeling. There are all the design choices. Someone needs to draw the plans, and you will need to review and revise the plans. Then, someone must go to the city and apply for permits and pay the fees. You will need to choose a contractor and plan the start of the project. Then, of course, there is the mess to contend with! You'll have demolition of your existing kitchen and/or bath(s). Will you want to live in the house while the work is being done? Are you prepared to eat all your meals out?

In summary, a remodeling decision is not to be taken lightly. It can pay off with significant reward if it is done well, but there is a cost for so doing. Think carefully, especially if this is your first remodeling project, and consider all of the ramifications of such a significant decision. It will have a cascade effect and so your timetable will need to be thought out very carefully.

There is also another school of thought about this. That is, the bigger the expense, the bigger the question as to whether it will be fully recovered in the sale price of the home. Moreover, what if you spend thousands of dollars to remodel the kitchen, and the new buyers decide that they don't like the granite you chose? What if they don't like the style of cabinets? What if your taste said black appliances were the hot items, but the buyer dreams of stainless steel appliances? What typically happens is that the buyer will try to discount the job so that they can replace what you've just done. In essence, they will want you to pay for it twice. If you follow the developer/design concept, this may not happen at all. It will not necessarily happen that way, but it does inject a new dimension into the negotiations. Anything that complicates the deal and moves the buyer further away from the table is not good for you, the seller.

There are exceptions to everything, of course. If you've bought the home to live in while you fix it, then a complete remodel may be what is in order, bathrooms, kitchen and all. They become business decisions based on the economics of the deal, and that is not the focus of this book. I'm more concerned with you, the homeowner who has lived in the home as your primary residence, and who is now ready to move, up, down or sideways.

Once you've set a budget to prepare your home for sale, you should consult with your realtor to go over the plan. Your realtor is your professional partner, and if you approach him in that way, he can be a valuable asset to you. Let your professional partner help you choose the best way to spend your money for the greatest return on your investment. If you need recommendations for trade's people to do the work you've agreed on, ask your agent for help. A good agent will have an extensive resource list to recommend. These are some of the reasons you are paying your realtor; to have an expert helping you, and to help you get the absolute maximum at the sale of your home.

One more important thing for you to do before you put your home on the market is to get rid of family photos! Pack them up and put them away. You can re-display them in your new home. Many buyers get sidetracked by photos. They may remember who they saw in the pictures and forget what the house looked like. They may know someone and get diverted, and in fact may not want to live in the house that so and so lived in. Photos complicate a deal and it behooves you to eliminate the distraction!

If your home is vacant, this presents another set of problems and opportunities. Vacant homes do not show well. Often there are few lights and the window coverings are shut, so the home looks dark and is dark. It can present a cold sterile and sometimes eerie environment. Unfortunately, many buyers do not have the imagination to furnish a vacant home and worry about how things will fit. A vacant home also opens the door for negotiation as buyers often think the seller must be desperate to sell.

One way to alleviate the problem of a vacant home is to "stage" the home. Furniture and accessories are rented and moved into your home. Companies that do staging employ interior designers whose job is to make your home look designer fresh and lived in. Staging is expensive, but the results are often worth the investment. I've seen many empty homes languish on the market for ages until they were staged. Once the staging was complete, the homes generally sold quickly, and for more money. Staging is a valuable tool for selling a vacant home for the most money and should not be overlooked when it is needed.

Finally, once you have decided what to do, prepare your home as quickly as possible. Remember that buyers come and go. When your home is ready to go on the market, you want to reach as many of the potential buyers as possible. You never want to hear that a buyer "would have loved this house, but just purchased another...if only it had been on the market sooner..."

Chapter 3:

<u>Choosing a Realtor</u>

How does one go about hiring a professional realtor? How does one choose who will sell what is probably the single most valuable asset any of us own? It is not an easy task, and much of the time it is done on blind faith and for reasons that do not involve careful decision making. There are many approaches to choosing a realtor, and I'll discuss several of the good and the bad. Ultimately, choosing the person to represent you is a very serious decision and should be given careful review and consideration. The decision can affect the amount of money you put in your pocket when the sale is completed and escrow is closed. It can affect the quality of the transaction. It can determine whether you work as a team with your realtor or view him as your enemy. Because so much is riding on the choice, I want to explore many of the dynamics.

First and foremost, choose a realtor who has a passion for the business. If the person is not passionate about what he does, run! The passion shows through personality and it is the extra ingredient that can make the difference between an extraordinary outcome and a mediocre one. Ask the agent you are interviewing why he sells real estate. What is the driving force? It should be to help people find their dream homes. It should be to incorporate their client's vision of what is important in a home and assist them in finding those attributes. The focus must be on you and your best interest.

Here are several "DO NOT's" in choosing a realtor. Do not choose a broker simply because he is passionate about making money. The broker may sell you down the river to secure his own paycheck, and that is the antithesis of what is good for you.

DO NOT choose a realtor because he tells you the price you want to hear. It's easy for a realtor to "pander" to your price requirements in order to secure your listing, even if he knows it's not a realistic price for the sale of your home. That same realtor is likely to come back to you and cajole you to lower the price. If fact, you can almost expect that to be the case if the all the evidence points to a lower value, but you still want to hear a higher number. A true professional realtor, who has your best interest at heart, will guide you to be realistic based on market conditions. Here's the "aha!" moment though. If together you decide to pursue a strategy that tests a higher than likely price, then you are both operating from the same reference point, and that's OK. When you're "duped" into thinking that you'll get the inflated price he quotes and you're choosing him as an agent because he's quoted that price then you may be sorry for your decision.

DO NOT choose a broker simply because he quotes you a low commission rate. In the chapter on Commission Philosophies and options, you'll read a great deal about commissions and how agents manipulate commission to work to your benefit or against your benefit. I think that after you read that chapter, you may want to rethink your emphasis on commission and look at how different levels of commission will affect your bottom line. It is not as simplistic as you may have been led to believe.

Be particularly aware of brokers who want to bring "clients" to see your house before you've given him a listing agreement. Many times, an agent eager to get your listing may ask you if he can bring a client to see your property. Unfortunately, you won't know if the "client" is a new associate or trainee, a colleague or a friend of the agent meant to "show" him your home and pretend they are prospective buyers. The agent may just be trying to impress you, by using a shill, to secure a listing on your property. At best, this is an unethical ploy to convince you of the agent's ability to bring buyers. It's really starting a relationship on false pretenses for the agent's selfish reasons, which certainly does not bode well for your long term relationship.

Let's begin with a global view looking at the big picture. Which brokerage firm best meets your needs?   Is it a large multi-national firm with offices and agents throughout the world? Is it a second tier firm, one not necessarily as large but still has a formidable presence?   How about a regional company with offices in a limited geographical area? Should you consider one of the local "boutique" agencies?

Begin by reviewing the benefits and disadvantages of each, starting with the large multinational companies.   The nation's largest residential real estate brokerage company has more than 1,000 offices, 64,000 sales associates and 9,000 employees operating in 35 major metropolitan areas.

Since they are the largest, they have many resources not available to smaller companies. For instance, one has a team of real estate attorneys on staff. The lawyers are corporate employees and are not paid hourly legal fees. They are available to agents through the managers in order to recommend solutions to potential problems with transactions. Since the lawyers are not "on the clock", they are available to deal with problems and the company is not imposing a time or budgetary limitation on them.

The largest of companies have an arsenal of marketing materials which are second to none in the industry. Their global purchasing power allows the continued improvement, enhancement and development of new and better materials. The ongoing effort to improve the marketing materials results in better ability to satisfy the needs of clients by increasing value to the consumer.

The oldest of the companies has over 100 years of experience. Corporate policies are well developed, thought through and refined as one might expect. Yet, for all its corporate culture, offices and agents have unique personalities, and operate in a pseudo-corporate environment with an entrepreneurial spirit. Thus, the biggest of companies can offer the best of all worlds. Experience, stability, well developed policies, extraordinary marketing, technology, flexibility and creative energy come together to offer sellers and buyers a first class experience.

Other brokerage companies are dramatically smaller by leaps and bounds. While some of them may be subsidiaries or related companies, many others are just not in the same league. Most brokerages do offer similar services, though none can rival the experience and size of the biggest. Mid level brokerage firms may do well for their clients, but do not have quite as many extensive services for their clients. If we refer back to the legal department discussion, smaller companies have outside counsel. When a problem arises, the cost of the solution is unknown. Other brokerage firms might have a tendency to spend very carefully (and perhaps foolishly) on outside counsel, so one may be short changed in the process.

Regional firms are constrained by the limits of geography and resources that are budgeted at relatively smaller levels. So, marketing materials, advertising and the ability to reach to a broad market audience may be limited. This can also be said for small boutique realtors. While the boutiques may have a mystique surrounding their names or influence, they are still small local companies with limited reach. So, it is important to carefully evaluate what you are selling, who your target market is, what kind and size of company will be best to market your property. These analyses and the decision you will need to make depend on the location of the property you are trying to sell, on the type of property you are trying to sell and on the price of the property. Local market conditions in your area will also play a role in your decision. If, for instance, you live in a very small market area and the local boutique realtor has the best reputation in town, then they may be the best choice for you. However, if you live in a large metropolitan area, you'll want to choose a company with the breadth and depth of the largest company in the marketplace.

Chapter 4:

<u>Understanding Your Realtor</u>

It is extremely important to understand the motivation of the agent you choose to represent you. I strongly believe there is only one valid reason to work in this business. That motivation must be to do what is in the best interest of the client! It's not a novel idea, and it's not money motivated. Yet, paradoxically, doing the right thing, the best thing for your client, ultimately results in significant monetary reward. I believe an enthusiastic and ethical approach to the purchase and sale of real estate should be the goal of all parties involved and that this ultimately results in smooth and successful transactions. Each one of my clients is important, and I'm driven to do an outstanding job for each.

I firmly believe that it is an honor and a privilege to help people fulfill their real estate goals, particularly in residential purchases and sales. It is gratifying and exciting to see people take their equity from one property and transfer it to another property which is better suited to their needs.   This is a business, when conducted professionally, ethically and responsibly, that is extremely gratifying!

Unfortunately, all too many agents just want a commission check and will do anything to earn that check.   And, I'm sorry to say, many will pressure you to accept an offer that is not in your best interest just to consummate a deal and generate a paycheck.   These agents give all of the ethical, responsible realtors a bad name.

Next, let's look at the individual real estate agent.   Many sellers get into trouble because they do not do their own research in choosing an agent to represent them.   Yet not doing the extensive research in the choice of an agent can be a costly mistake.   I'll explore the issue of commission in some detail in a later chapter, but for now realize that if one chooses the right agent, the commission paid is often an investment returned back to the seller from increased profits in the sale of the home.   The amount of commission is less important than the amount of money the sellers wind up getting.   In other words, it's the bottom line that should be paramount to the seller.   More about this will be addressed later.

What are the pitfalls in choosing an agent and how do many people make the choice? Where do they go wrong? How does choosing the wrong agent impact the process?

Too many people simply look at signs in their neighborhood and assume that if lots of signs are around, the agent must be good. That may or may not be the first mistake. There are many agents who are both very good and very busy and their signs are ubiquitous. However, not all are, and the number of transactions does not necessarily translate to the quality of the transaction or the level of service, professionalism, ethics or morality in the conduct of business. Many so- called prominent agents, those who may do one hundred or more transactions each year might be one of those who care more about turning inventory and collecting a paycheck than protecting your best interests.

There is also a sub-category of prominent agents. I like to call this type of realtor an "Ego-Agent". This person comes off like he knows it all, but is only out for himself and his commission. He's ego driven rather than service driven. He's more concerned with the chase to get the listing and the transaction than he is with the results of the transaction. It may be a numbers game with the Ego-Agent, that is, "how many listings can I get and how many can I process?" Rather, it should be about you and your needs and your goals. Watch out for the Ego-Agent! Hiring an Ego-Agent might cost you greatly when a transaction comes to the table. You'll get pressured to accept a deal and "convinced" the deal is in your best interest. Often, nothing could be further from the truth. Once again, a good agent will add value to the transaction and increase the sales price by virtue of how he positions your property in the marketplace.

And, be careful about simply saying "...(so and so) sold me the house, so I'll use him." If the agent is primarily a buyer's agent, he may not be the best choice for a listing agent. If the agent does not specialize in the area where your home is located, he won't be able to do a good job for you, because he won't be able to service your listing. The distance becomes a problem. He's working in a different area and can't get to your home easily. An out of area listing broker is often a major hindrance to selling a property.

Remember, this is a business decision for you and you should treat it as such. It's not personal, and a lot of money is riding on your decision. If you really feel strongly about involving your out of the area realtor, ask him to give you a referral to a quality agent who specializes in your area.

So, how does one choose an agent? Let's start the process logically and go through some of the steps that may help you choose a good agent.

One thing people do is to interview agents without letting them know you are interviewing them. One method for doing that is to visit open houses and chat with the agent holding the home open. Ask the agent questions. Do your own analysis of how the agent responds. Did the agent make you feel comfortable? Was he knowledgeable and warm? Did he treat you in the manner you want to be treated? Was he professional? Or was he condescending because he didn't think you were going to buy the property? Was he pushy and did he make you feel uncomfortable? Did he put you off? Pay attention to your feelings about that person.

Talk to friends, relatives and neighbors who have recently completed sales transactions. Interview them about their satisfaction from their transaction. Don't be afraid to ask tough questions and to ask around.

a. Did the agent deliver as much or more than promised?
b. Did the agent do a thorough job in presenting himself, his credentials and his marketing plan?
c. Had the agent followed through with his promises and executed the marketing plan he designed?
d. Was the agent accessible and available to you throughout the process to answer questions, or were you handed off to an assistant?
e. When the agent was unavailable and you left a message, did your call get returned within

an acceptable amount of time?

f. Did the agent attempt to be proactive and anticipate problems so that they could be handled expeditiously?

g. Did the agent bring you complete offers with all the information you needed to make an intelligent business decision? Was the contract complete? Did he request a pre-approval letter to be attached to the offer? Was there proof of funds for the down payment? Did the buyer supply any other information to help you come to a decision and was it included with the offer?

h. Did the agent discuss the offer with you and express an opinion as to the quality of the buyer?

i. If the offer was not up to your expectations, did your agent have creative options for your consideration and write a concise and thorough counter offer?

j. Were you satisfied with the final offer and did you feel that your agent represented your best interest?

k. Was the agent following up on due dates throughout the escrow? Did he demand that contingencies be removed when due?

l. Did you feel that the most important issue to the agent was commission and his own pay date?

m. How satisfied were you overall with the

performance of your agent?

These are some of the questions you should be asking your friends and relatives. Based on the answers, you may choose to interview one or more of the agents they recommend.

However, don't just take their word. Do your own checking and satisfy yourself that the answers are justified. When you interview each realtor, ask similar questions. Find out how they determine the price they recommend to you as the value of your home by asking about the process. The answers I would give you follow the questions, in "*italics*".

a. What research did you do to arrive at the value?

> *I do extensive research on a property to arrive at a value determination. Depending on the property and the area, I often prefer to ask a potential client for two appointments to discuss a market value for their home. On my first appointment, I visit with you and let you walk me through your home. I want to learn about your home through your eyes. I may want to take notes or digital photos as we walk through the*

house so I can review the details when I am back at the office doing research. Then, I search the MLS for all active, pending and sold properties in your area. Once I have the list of properties, I look at which ones are really comparable to your home. That analysis includes size of your home, style, amenities, lot size, condition of homes being compared, and upgrades. Then, I drive through the area and look at each home I believe is truly comparable to validate my opinion. Finally, based on the analysis, I come up with 3 prices. The high price is my educated opinion of the best case price. The second is the price at which I think you should list your home. The third price is the price at which I believe your home will sell in a reasonable amount of time.

b. How thorough is the research? Did you (Mr. and Mrs. Seller) feel that the value was accurate, documented, considered and well justified?

I'll spend several hours studying the information and carefully considering all of the data in order to give you the best possible opinion. Pricing is not only an analytical experience, but also an art. There are pricing strategies that we can discuss (see Chapter 10), each of which has certain advantages and disadvantages.

c. What commitment did the agent give you regarding advertising?

My marketing plan will be given to you in writing, committing to exactly what you can expect. You'll see which publications I'll use and when I'll run the ads. You'll know when brokers and public open houses will be held. The schedule will delineate the timeline for introductory postcards and brochures. You will know when we'll photograph your home and when we'll submit the listing to the MLS. In short, you will see my comprehensive marketing plan with all my activities outlined for you.

d. Which publications do you use for advertising and how often are the ads to be run?

Depending on the property, price and location, the publications may vary. At a minimum, I'll advertise your property in the Los Angeles Times. Your property will be advertised every week until we enter escrow.

e. Describe the type and number of photographs that are to appear on the MLS, the website and brochures.

I use professional quality photographs. The home will be prepared, staged if you will, for the photos to set a mood. Emotional photographs create desire and we want to create a strong desire for the property. We'll use a minimum of 10 photographs, and for some web sites, we'll use substantially more. Unfortunately, if you surf the web on real estate sites, you'll see all too often property that has no photograph or really awful photographs. Those properties will suffer for their agent's foolishness. Simply, people like looking at good photographs. People will remain on a website many times longer when there are multiple photos.

f. What kind of brochures would be used?

A professionally designed and printed brochure will be prepared

> *for distribution. And, a computer generated brochure printed on heavy stock paper will also be published for handout to agents and clients.*

g. Will the brochures be professionally printed, or merely office computer generated?

> *Yes. They will be both.*

h. Is there going to be a website presence? If so, what websites? How many?

> *Yes, there will be a strong web presence. In fact, your home will be presented on no less than 6-8 separate websites.*

i. How does the agent drive traffic to the websites?

> *There are several methods of directing attention to the various websites. Realtor.com, Coldwell banker.com, camoves.com, themls.com, latimes.com all do extensive media advertising. I personally maintain an advertisement on the latimes.com website which clicks through to my personal website. Every advertisement we publish will have at least one web address to reference.*

j. Will the website have a virtual tour of your

property?

> *Yes, I will have a professionally prepared virtual tour of your property that will be accessible from several websites.*

k. Does the agent have his own website and will your property be featured on the site?

> *I maintain 3 website addresses geared toward directing traffic to my website. They are, www.garykrieger.com, www.shermanoaksestates.info, and www.encinoestates.info. In addition, I have a web presence on www.camoves.com/gary.krieger and www.coldwellbanker.com.*

l. Does the agent have a lead capture system that directs prospects from the website to the agent?

> *Here's where Coldwell Banker is heads and shoulders above our competition. Its proprietary Lead Router® system captures every inquiry on the web. The lead will be transferred to me, if it is my listing, within 15 minutes or less!*

m. Is there a corporate requirement to respond in a specific timeframe before the lead is transferred to another agent for immediate response? What timeframe is that? It should be measured in minutes.

> *The company has a policy requiring all inquiries to be returned within 4 hours, maximum.*

n. How quickly does the agent find out about the inquiry and how fast does he respond?

> *Most calls are returned to potential buyers within minutes, and in no event later than a few hours. This rapid response time compares to a horrible industry average of 52 hours, if calls are returned at all.*

o. Is the agent going to conduct open houses for you, and will he do them personally?

> *I frequently hold my own open houses, unless there is a conflict in the open house schedule. In that eventuality, I will hand pick an agent competent to work at one of the open houses. I always conduct the broker open house myself. Sometimes I will have the assistance of another competent agent if we are working in a large home and we are expecting a large turnout of brokers.*

p. Will the agent walk through the neighborhood and speak to your neighbors about your home and invite them to an open house?

Absolutely yes! I will walk through your neighborhood and speak to every neighbor. If no one answers a door, I will leave information behind. Generally, I will knock on at least one hundred doors.

q. Will there be mailings to the general area announcing that your home is for sale?

Yes, a professionally printed, oversized postcard will be mailed to 500 to 1000 homes. The postcard will have at least one photograph of your home.

r. Will the agent personally speak to hundreds of other agents to promote your property?

In the local area, I will go to several affiliated offices and personally speak to several hundred agents and provide them with flyers on your property. Because of its size, often times a buyer is procured from within our network.

s. What kind of general advertising does the agent offer? How does that specifically benefit you?

My company has the largest advertising presence in the local newspapers in Los Angeles. Take a look and count the pages of advertising for CB versus other real estate companies. We dominate the market. You benefit from our overwhelming dominance because we control the most buyers. We have more pages of advertising, both color and black and white. We have more opportunities for special ad buys and often take advantage of extra inserts.

t. Is the agent regularly going to seminars to stay abreast of the market changes, generate new and refreshed ideas and continue his education?

This year alone, I have attended at least 100 hours of continuing education and seminars. I believe that an agent must continually learn in order to be at the top of his game. I gain new ideas for marketing and promoting properties at every seminar. New financing techniques benefit you also when that knowledge can help buyers qualify and obtain loans. Every time I attend a seminar, my goal is to find new ways to help you sell your property for the most money!

u. Does the agent have a broad background to

be able to assist in evaluating the many facets of an offer? Or, is he narrowly focused and without much experience?

> *I have an extensive business background wherein I have negotiated complex contracts for over 25 years. I've owned several businesses and purchased and sold real estate for over 35 years. My property management company has managed apartment and industrial buildings.*

v. Has the agent been through extensive negotiation training and certification?

> *Yes, in addition to my years of experience negotiating contracts in business and real estate transactions, I completed the prestigious Coldwell Banker Certified Negotiator program. I have read extensively about the negotiating process and practice theories proffered by the best negotiators.*

w. Will the agent be present for buyer inspections? Or, will an assistant be assigned to attend to the inspections?

> *I personally attend all inspections. Because I will be there, I can immediately know about any*

potential problems and become pro-active to resolve them. Conversely, knowing that no problems exist gives me one more tool to use in my arsenal to sell your home for the most money.

x. How does the agent respond to a question from other agents regarding the seller's motivation to sell?

The answer to this question is critical to the outcome. Typically, a seller's agent will respond that the seller wants to sell. He may give a price to the other agent which he knows will guide the other agent. But, this is a trap, and one to be avoided. Remember, your agent has a fiduciary responsibility to you. That responsibility includes doing everything for you, in your best interest. Since getting you the highest price possible for your property is in your best interest, how does giving another agent a lower price benefit you? Well, I'm here to tell you it doesn't! A question about seller motivation should be answered simply. For instance, the seller is moving because the family needs more bedrooms. Period. Often, an agent doesn't know when to stop talking. That can sometimes get in the way of the question!

By asking these types of difficult questions and evaluating the answers, you will be in a much stronger position to select the agent who best fits your expectations.

What does a full service agent do for you? I think this may be the most misunderstood aspect of real estate. Our profession has done a poor job of defining our role for you, and you may rightfully have the idea that we do very little to earn a substantial income. But, it's not as simple as you might have been led to believe.

Full service agents provide a variety of services and draw from a broad repertoire of talents. They need to be great listeners so that they learn what is important to you and what your goals are. We are part therapist, part business person, part clergyman and part social worker. We need to have analytical talents, business acumen and negotiation skills. We must understand how the pieces all fit together to form the whole. So, we need to coordinate financing and escrow, inspections and contingency removals. We must protect our sellers and make sure that proper due diligence is performed by all. We are marketing experts, advertising whizzes, mass mailing specialists and we fearlessly knock on doors of strangers to market property. We are promoters, supporters and cheerleaders. We need to have extensive knowledge of contracts and how to guide our sellers (and/or buyers) appropriately. We present offers and write counteroffers. We are negotiators. We need to verify and qualify buyers. We show and showcase property. We need to be accountable to our clients and available to answer questions. At times we need to be the bearer of bad news and we sometimes need to be confrontational, direct and blunt with sellers, buyers or other agents. We have a responsibility to be direct and forthright with our clients, and always do the right thing for them. We are web gurus and need to constantly update our web sites and our computer skills. We are networkers and researchers. And, while doing all of these tasks, we still need to run our own Real Estate business marketing ourselves, preparing budgets and organizing our own business affairs. We invest in your property, spending our money for advertising, brochures and signs without any guarantee that the investment will pay off with a sale and ultimately a commission. This is not a profession for the faint of heart nor the ignorant.

You should realize that if your home does not sell quickly, it will cost you money. Every month that your home sits on the market, you have expenses to maintain the property, including your mortgage, taxes and insurance. So remember, every decision you make will have an impact on your bottom line results. And the choice of an agent is again critical. A good agent can mean the difference between a quick sale and one that takes months longer to consummate.

If all the above is what a full service agent is, what is a limited service agent? Unfortunately, it can be anything less than a full service agent and most often is very limited. The range is from the agents and companies that help you sell your own property by placing your property in the MLS and then do little more, to those who are claiming to be full service agents but don't do half of what a real full service agent does. With limited service agents, you may have to conduct you own open houses and do your own property showings. Sometimes, the limited service agents will help you with contracts. The old saying, "you get what you pay for", certainly applies here. If you have the time to lead your own life, do your own job, and still have time to sell your own home, then perhaps a limited service agent will work for you. My experience is there are so many facets of this business and most sellers and buyers aren't aware of what is involved. Most sellers don't have the time or expertise to successfully do the job. I believe it is a false savings to use a low commission agent or agency, as again, it's the bottom line to the seller that really matters. If you save commission and walk away with less money, have you really saved? Of course not!

How does a full commission Realtor make you more money? He does it through the careful planning, marketing and positioning of your home to the right buyers. He does it through expert negotiation. He does it by understanding the motivation of buyers and finding solutions to allow a transaction to progress to conclusion. During every real estate transaction, there are dozens of pitfalls and opportunities for a deal to blow up and fall apart. A realtor's job is to use his skill to mitigate the problems and keep good deals moving forward. It's always a challenge and there are always issues that need to be negotiated throughout every transaction. Some are minor and others are major. But our job is to bring your deal to a successful conclusion. In a million dollar transaction, a 1% difference in commission is $10,000, which is certainly a lot of money. But, consider, if through his expertise and skill the Realtor is able to generate an additional $50,000 in an increased sales price, isn't the extra 1% worth it? I would suggest that an additional $40,000 in the sellers pocket is definitely worth the extra 1% commission. Think of this as an investment that reaps a 400% profit, generally in months, not years. So, the annual percentage rate on your commission investment is substantially higher. Personally, I'd like that kind of return every day of the week!

Different markets require different approaches to payment of commissions. When the real estate market favors buyers, it is more important to attract other realtors, who control the buyers, with a higher commission. If a broker is showing homes to a client, while ethics dictate he shouldn't consider commission, I've seen all too often that agents will take buyers first to homes with higher commission rates. Sometimes an increased commission can benefit the seller by producing a qualified buyer in a shorter period of time.

Chapter 5:

<u>Commission Philosophies</u>

What is the right amount of commission to pay your real estate agent? You have several options, each of which has its own supporters and detractors. Consider that commission, by and of itself, is generally not the issue.

Let's explore the full commission option. Generally, full commission is considered to be 6% of the sales price. But that's not always the case, and it varies by region. In many parts of the country, it is customary to pay 7% to the realtor. I recently attended a seminar given by one of the elite agents in the San Gabriel Valley in California who is recommending to his clients that they pay 8% in order to attract agents with buyers (this is in response to a market with a large inventory of homes that favors buyers).

First, remember what constitutes a full service agent. This is a full time profession which requires a great deal of skill in order to be done correctly. Those agents who take their responsibilities seriously deserve to be well compensated. As I discussed earlier, that compensation can pay large dividends to the seller and actually increase the sellers take away funds.

Top quality always comes at a price. There's a reason for that. Not all agents are equal and not all will deliver the same service and results. Analogies can be useful here. Consider automobiles. You can buy expensive, quality built cars and pay a premium for the luxury, service and utility. Or you can buy a "discount" car like a Yugo or Kia. Are they all cars? Yes. Will each get you to your destination? Probably they will. Is there a difference in the value? You bet there is. If transportation were the only criteria, a Yugo, or even a bicycle would suffice. Yet, many drive expensive and exotic cars. Why? Generally, the reason is that you are willing to pay for the best.

People who want the best service usually demand the best service. When they choose a physician or accountant or consultant, they pay a high fee for that professional's education, experience and outcome. Real estate is no different really. In fact, since your home is likely to be your greatest asset, the investment in a great real estate agent may be more important than your investment in most of the other professionals you use, with perhaps the exception of your doctor (after all, not everything is about the money)!

And, I dare say that most people do not negotiate with their attorneys, accountants and doctors. They earn their fees, they are entitled to their fees, and they deserve to be well compensated for what they do for you. So does your Realtor.

Do some agents negotiate their commissions? Sure. But consider this. An agent who gives up his money easily is more likely to give up your money easily also. If he is not willing to negotiate to protect his value in your transaction, what makes you think he will negotiate for you and fight for your money? Of course, not all agents who work for less than 6% are bad agents. But if they don't appreciate their own value, can they really be full service agents in the truest sense of the word? I think not. A one percent cut in commission from 6% to 5% represents a 17% cut in pay. Would you take a 17 % pay cut and still do as much? Maybe, depending on your value system and ethics, you would. Others may not. But there's more to it than that.

Realtors, even those of us affiliated with the largest of companies, are independent contractors and self employed. So, when I take on a project, I am the one who is investing my money to sell your home. And I do that without any guarantee that your home will sell. I am the one who pays for photography, brochures, virtual tours and signs. I am the one who pays for the advertising and marketing costs. These are expenses I incur in running my business. If you were to decide in the middle of the process that you don't want to sell after all, I may be out my investment dollars. Therefore, I am entitled to be compensated for my risk.   Marketing effectively costs a substantial amount of money. If an agent is to market your property diligently, his expenses can mount rapidly. Doing it properly is in your best interest. You want to sell as quickly as possible, and you want to sell for the most possible money.

When you ask your agent to work for a lower commission, realize that you are risking the bottom line outcome for yourself. Do you want to risk that an agent will, even unconsciously, lower the marketing budget for your property knowing that his own bottom line is going to be 17% lower? Undoubtedly, you will want full service, and be just as demanding, but the agent will still earn 17% less. That represents a one percent difference from 6 to 5%. Imagine going to a 4% commission and the effect that might produce.   In this case, 4% represents a 33% decrease in salary!   It's unlikely that you would accept that for yourself! But really, do you think that an agent with a substantially less marketing budget is going to provide the same exposure that a full service agent will provide?

Let's break this down further. Whatever the commission is, it will be divided between a listing office and a selling office. And, beyond that, the

Brokerage takes a percentage of the agent's gross commission.

I take pride in being a full service agent. For my fee, clients get full service and attention, dedication to the sale of their home, and total accountability to them for my performance. I suggest to them that they should consider how much they want to pay to the selling agent (the agent who procures the buyer). My recommendation is the more they pay the selling agent, the more likely they are to get more agents and buyers through their house. They are also more likely to get a good offer and to get it quickly. Of course, depending on the market conditions, the amounts paid to a selling broker may be more or less. In times when it is more of a sellers market, buyers' agents might charge less. But, when the markets change and it becomes more of a buyers market, you will want to offer a larger commission to the selling agent. Just as in any business, supply and demand govern prices. So, when buyers have abundant choices, a buyer's agent who stands to make a larger commission has a greater incentive to show your home to his client. It's simple economics really and it's a numbers game. The fact is, the more serious, qualified buyers who see your home, the sooner you will find the right buyer.

When the overall commission rate drops below 5%, the balance begins to tip away from the seller and the seller's best interest. When the profit motive is removed, less effort is expended, and the results may be relatively poorer. Just as when you buy other goods and services at a discount, the level of service drops. You get more service at Nordstrom; you get better quality and you pay higher prices than you do at Wal-Mart. I think most people understand the concept, but I don't think most have considered that the concept holds true across any industry or profession. It's just a simple business principle.

There are agents who devalue themselves, or certainly their services, and work for very little on a per transaction basis. I would recommend that you avoid them. I believe while you will get your home listed on the Multiple Listing Service, you will then get ignored. You may get an occasional advertisement. You may get an occasional open house. And you may get pressure to accept a low offer so the agent can move on to the next sale. He is working on volume at a discounted rate. But, who's really the loser here? The agent may be making a lot of money because of the volume. It's you, the seller who is probably going to get short changed. Focusing on the amount of commission, or the percentage, can be your worst enemy. Remember, the savings will be artificial if you don't get the maximum in return from your sale.

Once more, if an agent cannot or will not negotiate with you for commission, how do you expect that he will negotiate for you? You've already proven that you are a better negotiator than your agent!

Let's look at a typical discount broker's services. Once you're signed up and locked into a contract, you may get a phone call from your agent sounding something like this, "I have a conflict, can I send an agent/buyer over and will you show them your home?" On the surface, that doesn't sound so bad. But, home sellers are generally the worst people to have around buyers! Why? Because you oversell! You state the obvious. You point out the bathroom when the buyer is looking at a bathtub. You want to be in their faces to tell them everything wonderful you love about your home. As a seller, you are very emotionally attached to your property. The things you love about the property are the things you want to tell any prospective buyer. But, the general response I've seen from buyers is just discomfort and unease. Usually, owner showings are disastrous and the buyers run screaming from the house! And the worst thing is buyers often forget the house and only remember how uncomfortable they were feeling with the owner showing it.

When it comes to negotiating a deal for you, do you really believe your discount agent's agenda is the protection and maximization of your profits? If there is a problem during escrow, do you believe the discount agent will fight for you? Will the discount agent just roll over and put pressure on you to accept whatever the buyer is demanding so the agent can close the deal and get paid?

Like so many other professionals, we get paid for the results we deliver, not necessarily the time we spend to generate those results. The time is our risk, and some properties take a long time to sell. Marketing costs can be very expensive if the property sits on the market. Some properties sell quickly. Either way, the good realtor is doing his job. In most other businesses, the professionals are rewarded with a bonus if they exceed their goals. In real estate, sellers often think the realtor should be paid less if he succeeds quickly. But, since the realtor is the one who is taking the risk, he is entitled to the commission regardless of the length of time it takes to consummate a sale.

Here are some assumptions I think you should examine, suggested by Steve Shull, the former football star, of Performance Coaching. One assumption is that all agents are the same and perform the same service, regardless of the fee they charge. Another is that the home will sell itself. A third assumption is that the price is the price, period. Fourth, the property will get the same exposure regardless of who lists it.

So, here are some questions you should ask yourself. Do you believe all agents are the same? Do you believe that an agent who will earn substantially less will give you the same service as someone who is truly a full service agent? Do you believe the price of your home is going to be the selling price and that through proper positioning, a good agent cannot influence the price or get a higher price? Do you really believe someone earning less will spend money equally with someone earning more to market your property? If you have a marketing budget and someone else has half the budget, do you think your property will get the same exposure?

While you may be focused on getting a discount on the commission, I would suggest that your focus is misplaced. Truly, I believe your focus should be on maximizing the approximately 93% of the sale proceeds you will walk away with when the transaction is finalized. And, that's what you get with a professional full service agent.

The good news is when you choose the best agent, the commission becomes a secondary issue. Your agent should make you money, not cost you money, regardless of the commission. Just be sure to choose wisely and carefully, because that choice will determine whether you will have gotten your return on your commission investment.

Chapter 6:

<u>Marketing Your Home</u>

Developing a marketing plan for you is a key project that your full service broker will provide. Ideally, he'll provide you with a timeline showing what will happen, and when.

As I discussed earlier, before your property comes onto the market, there is a lot of preparation to be done. Among other things, the home needs to be staged for sale. Some landscaping may need to be done. Photographs need to be taken. A virtual tour may need to be ordered.

The most important issue is when your home is presented to the market for the first time, it must be done right. If it's not, it will be hard to recover. The home will be seen as "less than", and that will be the impression that the agents will remember.

I can't tell you how many properties are presented to the market and don't even have a single photograph show up on the MLS system.

That means there are no photographs to showcase the property on the websites. Or, photos may appear on the MLS turned sideways or upside down! This is just plain stupid, sloppy, and the agent doing that should be fired on the spot! A good agent knows that and will make sure that every detail is proper and ready for input. He will never release a property for showing until it is ready to be shown. Doing anything else is a slam dunk way to reduce interest in your property and reduce your bottom line! It doesn't matter to me if it takes a week or if takes a month to get your property ready for showing. Your agent should advise you how to do it right.

So, now that your property is ready to be introduced to the marketplace, what is scheduled to happen? Well, you should have been shown the plan which includes the advertising schedule, the broker's open house schedule and dates for public open house. Your realtor should inform you when he'll send postcards announcing your property for sale and when he is going to canvas your neighborhood. He should let you know when printed brochures will be available for distribution and when networking will be done to promote the property and how. These are just some of the issues that will be included in your agent's marketing plan.

Every marketing plan will be somewhat different. Depending on the many factors relating to the home, the advertising requirements may be varied. But in any event, some basics should be standard.

The major local newspaper will be the prime candidate for most of the local advertising. The specifics of the property will determine exactly what form the advertising will take. At a bare minimum, the box ads, in black and white will be run regularly. Color box ads should be part of the ad mix as well. And, open house announcements should be included in Saturday or Sunday newspaper insertions. Also, local real estate magazines may be candidates for ad placement. The frequency and placement should be discussed and rationalized. Sometimes, more than one edition or newspaper exists in different areas of a city. Ads may be placed in those newspapers also to broaden the exposure. Unique approaches to advertising set homes apart from the rest and direct attention away from the ordinary and toward the unique.

Some properties demand specialized advertising be placed. There are magazines for real estate. There are magazines for special interests and architectural display. For instance, an architect designed property would benefit from specialized magazine advertising. Generally, glossy color ads with multiple photographs and professionally written copy should be considered. Often, these magazines have a 1 to 2 months lead time for publication and will remain on display for an additional 1 to 2 months. In a seller's market, where homes are sold quickly, there may not be the time for this specialized advertising. In slower markets with higher inventory, these may be perfectly appropriate. In fact, in slower market times, a property may be expected to incubate on the market for 90 days or more, and thus the specialized advertising is even more valuable.

The website placements require some thoughtful consideration. How will the copy read? In what order should the photographs be placed? How many photographs? Is a virtual tour included and has its placement been coordinated with the videographer? With at least 6 to 8 websites to be coordinated, a good deal of thought needs to go into the decisions and all the paperwork needs to be done.

Networking will be a major undertaking. Networking takes the form of personal visitation to hundreds of other agents. Some of this contact will be one on one with the agents most likely to have a client for a specific property. Other network contact will take the form of personal announcements made at real estate office meetings and brochures being distributed to those agents. These network meetings may be within several offices of one company and meetings with agents from competing companies. In addition to personal contacts via telephone, e-mail blasts can reach hundreds or thousands of agents.

I believe it is a sound business practice to market to as many groups of people and types of people as possible. The more people who see a house, the sooner one is likely to find the right buyer. Exposure is the key to marketing. One more group I like to expose to your property is your neighbors. I think it's good for them to attend an open house, and will encourage them to do so. Neighbors are often reluctant to come to your open house not wanting to appear nosey. I mail announcements to the neighbors informing them of the listing. And, I will go door to door and speak personally to the neighbors and invite them to see the house. Public relations and an open invitation can go a long way toward encouraging referrals from your neighbors to their friends and relatives who may be interested in purchasing your house.

Real estate is cyclical and just like the stock market, it has some ebbs and flows. During the periodic recessionary times, as in the early 1990's, good agents were still helping their sellers realize the maximum sales price for their homes. Creative and out-of-the-box marketing strategies can pay substantial dividends. Sometimes offering to pay for a buyers closing costs can bring a buyer who is otherwise qualified, but may be interested in conserving cash. In a market where interest rates are rising, a seller may offer to buy down a loan rate for the buyer, thus easing the mortgage payments and attracting a buyer who otherwise might have trouble qualifying. There are countless ways to motivate buyers and it behooves the seller to consider any realistic option available to him. It is not always necessary to begin with expensive or outrageous incentives to attract a buyer. If a home lingers on the market though, it may be time to become more aggressive. The incentives may end up being less costly than another type of price adjustment and a cost-benefit analysis should help make that determination.

Marketing is one of the two most important aspects of selling your home. If marketing is done effectively, and the home is priced correctly, all other things being equal, the home will sell. If the home doesn't sell, and the marketing has been thorough, then the price of the home is likely too high and the market is sending that message. In the final analysis, it is principally marketing and price that influence the sale.

Chapter 7:

Pricing Strategies

So what's the best way to price a home? The answer varies, and there is no one right way. Each home is different. Each neighborhood is different. And each seller's needs are different. So, there are a lot of factors that influence the "right" pricing strategy. And, there is as much art to pricing as there is science.

The starting point is looking at comparable sales. Of course, with expensive, trophy properties, there may not be any comparable sales. Generally those homes break new sales records for price. But, that's a different discussion, and here the focus will be on homes that are not above the very top end of the market.

In addition to the comparable sales, one needs to look at the competition. When looking at the comparable homes, are they really comparable? Is the view as good? Have the improvements been compared? Are there adjustments for the variables and differences within a comparable group? How many homes are on the market? Is it a buyers' market, a sellers' market or a balanced market? What are the trends in the marketplace, both generally for the region and specifically for the immediate area? How long is the average home remaining on the market before sale? What's the pulse of the market and the mood in general?

What are the needs of the seller? It may seem obvious that every seller wants to sell for as much as possible. But beyond that, is the seller in a hurry? Have they purchased another home and need a sale to complete the transaction? Does the seller have funds to purchase the other home and carry the home for sale for an extended period? Is the seller willing to just sit tight and wait for an offer?

Are there problems with the property? And if so, are those problems fixable or not. For instance, a fixable problem is an overgrown front yard that can be cleaned up. A problem that is not fixable is a home that backs up to an industrial building or a freeway. Having a problem that isn't fixable means that the property price may need to be adjusted, discounted if you will, to reflect the defect.

So, answers to the questions may be necessary in order to evaluate the best pricing approach. When a home is priced at the low end of the expected sale range, multiple offers may bid the price up higher. A home priced lower than expected will attract attention and may thus generate several interested buyers. If a seller is in no big hurry, a price at the higher end of the range may be justified.

The important concept is that there is no one right strategy. The careful and reasoned questioning of the sellers should help clarify the correct option. The discussions between the sellers and the realtor should lead to the right price. Of course, in the final analysis, the agent can only recommend the pricing approach. The seller is the ultimate decision maker. It is important to remember that the goal of the process is the sale of one's home. Sometimes the goal is lost like the proverbial "can't find the forest for the trees". Sellers sometimes become so attached to a preconceived notion of value that they fail to recognize the market is speaking to them.

A seller and real estate agent must come to terms with the price. If a home is priced too high, and a seller is insistent that the price is what he wants, then the agent must decide whether he wants to take the listing. Or, the agent may decide that the property is not likely to sell and therefore has no interest in spending a great deal of marketing money to promote a property that has little likelihood of selling.

If the sellers insist that a particular agent be the salesperson to list his home, then they would be well advised to reach a mutual agreement about pricing strategy. One successful method is for the broker to try the seller's price for a couple of weeks to a month, or some other mutually agreed term. If the home isn't shown much, and if there are no offers within 2 – 4 weeks, then the seller will agree to a predetermined price reduction to an agreed upon level. In this way, the seller gets to test his price. If he's correct, then everyone wins. If his price is above the market, then the realtor can adjust the price to a realistic market level.

One caution though is that sellers must take bold and decisive reductions to price the property at the correct market level if a reduction is to be done. Small, incremental reductions should be avoided and are really to the seller's detriment, as the seller will constantly be "chasing" the market down in a cool market. The effect of that is the seller's home becomes the sales tool for other agents to sell other, more reasonably priced homes in the area. Your high price makes other comparable homes look even more enticing. It is self-defeating for the seller to do that.

In summary, there are 3 strategies for pricing. You can price high and hope the market will buy. You can price your home at the expected market price and be right on the market. Or, you can price the property under the market, and hope to generate multiple offers to bid the price up.

Chapter 8:

Broker and Public Open Houses

A home is usually introduced to the market by a Broker's Open House. Careful preparation for the open house is a must, and a rush to market before the home is ready to be shown can be a very costly mistake. Once the home is ready, the agent will inform the brokerage community and invite them to attend an open house.

While it may seem apparent, some people do not pay attention to the importance of a Broker's Open House and the brokerage community. Over 70% of homes nationwide are sold by a realtor. In many metropolitan areas, the percentage is much higher. It is most likely that another real estate broker will be the one to bring the buyer who will eventually purchase your home. So, the broker you choose to represent you had better work well with the brokerage community in general.

Some agents have good karma and do the right thing all the time. These agents have the respect and recognition of their peers, and other brokers appreciate working with them. Other agents have reputations as bad agents, unreliable or unethical agents. Some have very abrasive personalities, bad tempers and can be annoyingly abusive. This behavior may result in a deal falling apart, because the broker cannot successfully handle the challenges associated with the sale. Be careful not to choose one of these people as your listing agent. Other agents don't want to work with these types of realtors, and you may lose a deal because a good agent won't bring a buyer to see a property listed by one of the types of people described above.

Most of the time, the good real estate agents in an area attend broker open houses. Every week, there is a "caravan" when brokers tour the homes that are newly listed in an area. The homes represent the available inventory, so it behooves agents to attend these open houses.

However, it is not always as easy as it would seem to be to get the brokerage community to attend open houses. So, sometimes bribes need to be employed! Food is a great bribe and so, often, I'll serve or cater a meal at the open house. The right atmosphere, the food and well prepared marketing materials are essential to a successful property introduction.

Depending on the home, and the circumstances surrounding the marketing of a home, a catered lunch, dinner or other party may be indicated. Generally, the more expensive the property, or the more difficultly expected in selling a property, the greater the creativity required to grab the attention of the brokerage community.

Just as broker's open houses draw the real estate community, public open houses draw buyers. The same care in preparation must be observed to make the most of each open house.

Brokers have different philosophies regarding the frequency of open houses and how to conduct an open house. I believe public open houses should be held to showcase the property to buyers. However, frequent open houses can send the wrong message to buyers. Guidelines though have variations, and sometimes more open houses are better for a seller in attempting to attract a buyer. The seller and realtor should discuss the pros and cons of holding open houses, the frequency of having them and the cost-benefit ratio. That ratio involves homeowner preparations, time spent out of the house during the open houses, and the benefits versus the inconvenience.

When conducting an open house, some brokers feel fervently that people who attend the open house must sign an attendance sheet, a register, and provide name, address, phone number and e-mail address. Those brokers who insist, may ask a guest to leave if they don't sign in. Other brokers ask, but don't insist that the guest sign in. And, another group of brokers feel that it's intrusive to ask someone to sign a register and they don't bother to ask.

I find that people resent being pressured into signing a register. And worse, when forced to do what someone doesn't want to do, false information is generally entered. So, why press the issue? Well, many brokers feel that while they are holding a home open, anyone who attends is a possible new client and they want to "capture" that potential client. Some also want to send them a thank you note for attending and to add those people to their mailing list.

At the other end of the spectrum are brokers whose philosophy is if a visitor wants to let the broker know their name or contact information, they will volunteer it. If they don't want to engage in conversation or sign in, they most likely are not serious and would not be potential clients anyway. Those brokers think there is no reason to start the relationship on an adversarial basis. Both methods, or something in between, provide a successful approach, and it may have more to do with the broker's personality, and what he's comfortable doing.

While public open houses don't often sell homes, sometimes they do. The public open house also provides an opportunity for neighbors to see what is transpiring in their neighborhood. Sometimes neighbors have friends or relatives who may want to move to the neighborhood, and they are previewing the home for them.

As with all decisions in the sale of real estate, there are benefits to consider with each option. In the case of open houses, generally they are beneficial. However, there are inconveniences to the seller. Often, decisions to hold open house may depend on the life style of the seller and the willingness of the agent to hold the house open.

Chapter 9:

Home Safety & Protection

This topic is of extreme importance. We become complacent and think nothing untoward will ever happen to us. So, please remember that each us needs to be mindful of our personal safety. It is amazing to me that people will be so cavalier with their personal valuables and jeopardize their personal safety.

In preparation for putting your home on the market, everything of significant value should be packed up and put away. If you own valuable jewelry, it should be put into a safe or safe deposit box. Small items that are valuable and that can be easily pilfered by people touring the house should be put away or locked up. Personal records, financial records, check books and credit cards should be secured.

If you don't have a place to put your valuables, make arrangements with a relative, or a trusted friend to keep some of your belongings. Please don't jeopardize your valuable and cherished possessions because you didn't think to put them away. Unfortunately, not everyone who visits your home will have the same values and ethics you do. Items of personal property, on occasion, disappear.

I recently agreed to help out another broker and held 2 open houses for her. At the first public open house, I had to hide the homeowner's personal effects to safeguard the owner. The owner left the premises and left his wallet with all his credit cards, his checkbook, a couple hundred dollars in cash and various other items on the kitchen table. I don't believe the owner intentionally left those items, yet he didn't think to take them and he risked jeopardizing his identity, credit and cash.

At another open house, the owner left a house key and her car keys hanging on a key rack in the hallway next to the garage door. The keys were within easy reach of anyone who wanted to take them. I was apparently more concerned with protecting their safety than they were. No doubt, these were simple oversights, but they could have been extremely dangerous ones. I take great care in advising my clients about protecting their valuables.

A second important consideration is personal safety. It is imperative that one be attentive during open houses, as not all people who come through are on the up and up. They may want to case the home for future robbery, or they may want to harm the residents or agents. It is better to have the agents show the property, and to ascertain the identity of anyone claiming to be a real estate agent. Common sense must prevail, and preventive measures must be taken.

Chapter 10:

<u>Qualifying the Buyer</u>

Getting a buyer to step forward and make an offer to purchase your home is great. But, if the buyer is not qualified for a purchase at the level of your home price, it is just a waste of your time. Moreover, it can be psychologically defeating for the seller to think he has a buyer only to find out it's not true.

So, qualifying potential buyers before that person makes an offer makes real sense. Your realtor's job is to make sure a buyer has the wherewithal to fund a down payment, the credit to get a loan, the income to support the loan he needs and other pre-qualifications certified by a competent mortgage broker. If your agent is acting as a dual agent and representing the buyer as well as the seller, he'll want to do these checks right away. If the buyer has another agent, your agent's job will be to question the other agent to ascertain that all the information is available before an offer is written.

Once you know that a buyer has the ability to complete a purchase, you can begin to put a deal together. This is where the negotiations get started, and statements made by the listing broker can impact the price positively or negatively. It's just one more reason why choosing your agent is such an important decision.

Chapter 11:

Reviewing Offers

Your agent will bring you the offers he receives for your property. It is his job to review the offer with you and point out all the issues that will affect the outcome of the sale. These issues may be positive or negative, but each will have an impact.

Careful review, thoughtful consideration and reasoned evaluation will help generate a response. The response may be an acceptance, a rejection or a counteroffer. If the offer to purchase your property was submitted at full price and without contingencies, you may accept the offer as it was presented. However, this is rarely the case, and more often than not, it requires some action other than simple acceptance. For instance, the buyer may have asked for a longer contingency period than you are willing to give. Or the buyer qualifications may not have been adequately documented, so the loan provisions of the contract may need further development, tightening or clarification before signing the agreement.

When you are dealing with a multi-page contract, the Purchase Agreement and Joint Escrow Instructions, there are possible issues on every page of the contract to review. Diligence and detailed analysis is the only way to proceed. Since we are in such a litigious society, all the more care is required. It is your realtor who has the job of helping to keep you out of trouble and hopefully steering you away from lawsuits. While nothing can prevent someone from filing a lawsuit, a transaction where all the "i's" have been dotted and all the "t's" have been crossed is one that is less likely to be litigated. However, sloppy work on the part of the agent can open you to legal action as well as expose the agent and his broker to liability. Strong policies and procedures to review and protect the interests of all the parties involved becomes not only necessary, but the ethical thing to do.

Chapter 12:

Negotiating the Offer

One of the most vital services I provide for my clients is to be a fierce, assertive and when necessary, aggressive negotiator. Negotiation is one of the things your realtor can do for you that can make you tens of thousands of dollars extra. The skills your realtor uses on your behalf can pay his commission many times over and net you significantly more money in the process. If your agent is trained and experienced, perhaps a Certified Negotiation Specialist or a graduate of the prestigious Certified Negotiator Program, and is working in your best interest, the details of the deal can tilt significantly in your favor.

I have read extensively about negotiation and have attended seminars and taken courses on negotiation. I have attained the Certified Negotiator designation. My 26 plus years in business included negotiating all sorts of contracts including long term purchasing contracts, sales contracts, employment contracts, leases and industrial real estate purchases. Vast experience in negotiation brings a knowledge base that can be applied to benefiting my clients in hammering out the best possible deal. Make sure that your agent can boast extensive negotiating credentials. Anything less will cost you money.

This is important. Just because you work with a "top agent" doesn't mean that your agent will doing what is in your best interest. Many top agents work on volume, and the key to volume is turnover. If getting your property listed and sold quickly is the only criteria for the agent, then you may get cheated out of possible additional sales dollars. There are "top" agents whose discount commissions are discounted for a reason. If you've chosen a discount service agent, you shouldn't expect that when it comes to negotiating for your money the agent won't discount that portion of his service as well.

Ask yourself this question. If an agent is closing 100 – 200 or more deals a year, how does he have time to finesse the details of your sale? He may have a staff to help, but that is not the same as having the agent you choose do the work! You hired this "top agent" because of his being a "superstar". But, if you are handed off to assistants for most of the process, have you really done yourself a service? And, at 100-plus deals per year, recognize it's not about you, it's about the agent, the agent's ego and his money. Remember the discussion earlier about the "Ego-Agent"?

There are many different styles of negotiators. One must recognize and understand the opposing negotiator's style. Negotiators can be analytical and they will ask one question after another. They want to know everything and will follow up every question with another question. The good news is that the analytical negotiator is generally rational and will come around once a case is made for the position, as long as the facts warrant the conclusion. There are those who negotiate by intimidating. These people usually yell and scream. They are always threatening to walk away. They frequently take a negative position, "...it will never happen..." And the intimidators rarely listen to what is being said to them. They want to engage in battle and they are great at arguing! So, the best way to work with an intimidator is to remain calm, focused and not to engage them with dramatics. It drives the intimidator nuts, because they can't get you going. And eventually, they will stop their silliness and get down to business. There are many other types of negotiation styles, of course, and combinations of many styles. While generally, one personality type exists and is dominant, sometimes they are mixed. Each of these types of personalities requires a different approach to helping facilitate a deal. What works with an analytical negotiator is likely to stall negotiations with an intimidator, so careful assessment of the negotiating counterpart is essential. Remember, there are countermeasures to deal with every type of negotiation style, and each must be used appropriately to achieve the best outcome.

Let's focus on the negotiation process. One of the functions of the negotiator is to care about the outcome, but not to be emotionally involved. The negotiator who is willing to walk away from a negotiation generally comes out on top. The side with the tightest time deadlines will often concede the most.

Herb Cohen is generally acknowledged to be one of the foremost negotiators in America. He has written "Negotiate This, By Caring But Not T-H-A-T Much" and "YOU CAN NEGOTIATE ANYTHING". In his books, he writes that negotiation should be approached from a positive position. There is an art to knowing when to remain firm, when to give away something, and when to walk away. These are skills good negotiators learn. They apply those skills in order to make the best deals for their clients. It takes knowledge, experience and patience to be a good negotiator. Don't expect Ego-agents to have the time or the patience to do the best job for you, and that will cost you money. Done properly, a savvy negotiator will make you a lot of money in the transaction.

Mr. Cohen says negotiations should begin on a friendly, cooperative basis. Since, in polite society, like often begets like, it's always better to start off in a cooperative spirit. The approach you take to negotiating can have a more significant result than what you're talking about. In other words, by listening attentively, unrushed, and considering the value of the other's worth and benefit, the stage will be set for what follows. By doing so, we affect emotions, expectations, rapport and trust. From this base, it's easier to progress and engage with the other side. It is always easier to move from this cooperative spirit to one of more rigidity. If one begins with a hardnosed and rigid position, and later must back down, that negotiator loses credibility. Loss of believability ultimately weakens his negotiating position.

Don't confuse behaving politely and approaching negotiation in a civilized manner for weakness. If anything, it is just the opposite. Think about a sports metaphor. It begins in a gentlemanly fashion with cordiality and a handshake. Then the rallying begins. Catch your opponent off guard and he loses. Set up your strategy, keep your opponent guessing, exploit his weakness and go in for the win! The process works and my clients benefit from my many years of broad negotiating experience. You need to accept nothing less than great skill in this area, or you may lose a lot of money.

Remember that negotiation means compromise. If both sides are willing to give away something (and not necessarily something of great value) for a positive result, a win-win situation exists. That is not to say one just gives away the store! In fact, good negotiators get their clients much more for their property by applying sound negotiating principles.

In a neutral market, a win-win situation doesn't mean that everyone is happy with the outcome. In fact, the sign of a good deal may be that each of the parties feels like he's given a bit too much. If both sides are a bit unhappy, that's usually a good sign! Often times, the seller will say "I could have gotten more..." and the buyer will say "I should have paid less..." In a strong seller's market, the dialog may change. The seller may say "I can't believe I got so much for my home" and a buyer might say "Hooray, I was the successful bidder and I got my home..."

Negotiation does not stop when an offer is accepted and escrow is opened. Until the escrow closes, there are opportunities for the parties to get into further negotiations. This happens as a result of home inspections. Further negotiations may happen due to reports from geologists and termite inspectors. Things come up; preliminary title report and easement issues generate another opportunity for the buyer to reach into your pocket and pull out more of your cash! And again, a discount selling agent who isn't looking out for your best interest is likely to pressure you to accept concessions. He wants your escrow to close quickly and without the extra work required to protect your money!

You shouldn't come away from this thinking that a good agent will never concede any money or terms, as that is not the reality of negotiation. Of course, there generally must be some give and take. Rather, your representative should use his best discretion and skill to continually maximize the benefit for you.

Every objection has a reason, but usually the reason given is not the real reason or the stumbling block. A good negotiator will get to the truth, and find a solution that resolves the real reason for the request to take your money. To a good negotiator, every nuance can be addressed and can work to your advantage. The issue may have started as a request for a discount in sales price for some stated reason. But, if the truth is discovered, a non-monetary solution may satisfy the buyer. Getting to the truth though often takes time. So, be patient and help your agent get you the best sales price and terms he can get.

In summary, there are no shortcuts to hard ball negotiations. Negotiations must be finessed in most cases, perhaps with the exception of significant difference in the abilities of the negotiators. In that case, the win can be easy and quick. Generally, a battering ram approach is just as counterproductive as rolling over and losing. One needs to be tough, single minded, forceful and assertive.   Yet, the greatest successes in negotiation occur when those characteristics are tempered with a business-like manner, professional, and perhaps deceptively easy going approach masking the tough intentions of the serious, experienced negotiator.

Chapter 13:

Integrity

Finding an agent with integrity may be the hardest part of your decision. The success of your sale, and the amount of profit you are likely to make, can be directly affected by the integrity of your agent. If your agent has your best interest at heart, then you don't need to worry about your bottom line. You won't be negotiating with your agent against yourself to get your home sold. But if your agent is more concerned about counting his commission, then you have a problem.

So how do you determine someone's integrity, and values? There is no easy answer and sometimes it's a gut feeling. But ask questions. Talk to the real estate office manager. Talk to past clients the agent has worked for and ask them for references. In other words, again, do your own due diligence. Spend the time to do the research and remember that you are dealing with a choice related to what is likely to be your greatest asset.

Here is an example of how your agent can cost you a great deal of money. It is all too common for a buyer's realtor to ask a selling agent, "Is the seller very motivated and what do you think they will take?" And, just as often, the selling agents response is, "Oh, they're very motivated and I think they will take $____" (some number well below the listing price, perhaps 10's or 100's of thousands of dollars less). That type of response will cost you more thousands of dollars than you want to think about.

An agent with integrity remembers he works for his client. His job is to protect his client's interests and do the best job for his client. He will respond very differently in an effort to move the offering price up from the beginning. Remember, your agent should have helped you begin the negotiating process when you hired him to list your home. Everything he recommended to you should have been designed to increase the value of your home. So, to the same question, your agent might respond, with a chuckle and a twinkle in his eye, "I don't know their bottom line number, but I'm sure if your client offers more than the list price, they will give the offer the consideration it deserves!". "Seriously, here are the comparable sales that justify the price we are asking, and my client's home has these additional amenities, etc...they are asking a fair price..." With this answer, your broker is not tipping his hand, even if he knows the seller's bottom line. Your full service agent, in this instance, is moving the buyer up in price by reinforcing the value you've created. The other agent is left thinking that if his client writes an offer that is too low, he won't get a favorable response. That leaves him in the position of advising his client to make the best opening offer to start the dialog. This is just one example of what your broker should be doing to protect you and help you get the absolute most you can get for the sale of your home.

Integrity will make the difference between a broker who will sell you out for a quick deal, and one who will always put your best interest above his own. Please do not think for a moment that all brokers are the same. It does matter who you choose. Your choice will earn you or lose you thousands and thousands of dollars. So, if your cousin Vinnie just got into real estate, think carefully about whether he's the right professional to handle your sale! He may save you a few dollars in commission, and cost you many times more because of what he left on the negotiating table. Or, if the amount of commission you pay is your only criteria in hiring an agent, you may be doing yourself an enormous and costly disservice.

Offers, counteroffers and acceptances can be a trying time for sellers and buyers. There are many details that need attention and the waiting game as contracts go back and forth can be anxiety producing. Patience is often the best strategy. The process takes on a life of its own, and with the skilled help of your agent, you can achieve the best result.

Chapter 14:

Escrow

Escrow is simply an unbiased company that handles all the paperwork and money for all the parties. They don't work for the seller and they don't work for the buyer. The job of escrow is to follow the instructions you've given in your sales contract and to be certain that all parties have complied. They are not enforcers, rather safe havens for each party to protect the money placed in escrow and to preserve title until the proper time for change in title. The escrow office is not concerned whether something is fair, but only that the contractual obligation is acknowledged and followed. Escrow has a fiduciary responsibility to both the buyer and the seller to follow the instructions and protect the interest of each party until all conditions for the sale can be completed.

The escrow company maintains a trust bank account and all monies related to the transaction will be held in trust for safekeeping. When all requirements of the escrow have been completed, then the Escrow Officer will prepare a summary of all the costs charged to, and credits for, each party, and disperse the funds held in trust to the parties as indicated by the closing statements. They are responsible to you for assuring you receive exactly the amount of funds from the transaction to which you are entitled.

Let's go back to the opening of escrow. You finally have a signed contract and it's time to open escrow. You may think that the hard part is over and your home is sold. Unfortunately, the time ahead is fraught with roadblocks and pitfalls as well. Some escrows go very smoothly and proceed without a hitch. Others are very difficult and require the knowledge, skill and professionalism of your realtor to overcome the obstacles.

Throughout the escrow, your agent needs to follow up with details. Are the buyers proceeding with their due diligence? Have the inspections been scheduled? Is the loan processing proceeding and on track? Has the seller provided all the disclosures to the buyer? Are there reports, old or new, in the possession of the seller that need to be given to the buyer? Your agent needs to advise you to turn over copies of all the records and receipts from home repairs, improvements, and to disclose any and all problems about which you have knowledge.

Your broker needs to follow up to be certain

that contingencies are removed by the dates required in the contract. If the dates are not being met, why not and what else needs to be done to keep the process moving. The negotiations may never stop, and your agent needs to be there for you to protect your interests at every step.

Once you are in Escrow, you'll have countless more papers to sign, as if getting through the Sales Contract, Counteroffers, Disclosures and Amendments weren't enough! Your agent should be available to you to answer your questions and explain what you are signing and why you're being asked to sign. For experienced sellers who are familiar with the paperwork, this may not be an issue. But for a seller who hasn't sold a property in a long time, this is really important.

You may need to be advised by other professionals, such as lawyers and accountants as well, during the process, and if you have any questions, you should immediately consult with them. It may be to your advantage to speak with your attorney about issues that affect your legal rights. You might need to speak with your accountant about tax implications of the transaction. Sometimes issues arise with land use planning or lot splits, and the need for a Planning Consultant may arise. These are just a few of the issues with which you may need assistance. But your broker should be there for you to help with the process.

Your agent becomes your expert triage person. He can advise you of the types of consultants you might want to contact. Or, you may want expert advice and your agent might have a list of consultants in that field to suggest.

In fact, our company has its Concierge Service. The Concierge division is a referral service to refer you to pre-screened and reference checked people to solve your problem. And, the company stands behind the work of the people they recommend. This is a valuable service that may not be similarly available from other real estate brokerages.

Assuming that you've gotten through the escrow process, it's about time to close escrow. Final signatures may be needed on certain documents. The escrow agent will let you know what is finally needed to complete the transaction.

Closing escrow is usually a very happy day! If the Realtor's have done their job correctly and with integrity, all the parties should be content. I realize it doesn't always work out that way, but it is the goal. The seller has achieved his goal and will receive his check from escrow for the proceeds representing all his net equity in the property. The buyer will hopefully be excited to own his new home and anxious to begin moving in.

Chapter 15:

Transition

Of course, before the buyer can take possession, the seller needs to move out! Most of the time, sellers will be packed up, the moving truck comes and they leave. Hopefully, the goodwill of the buyers and sellers will help the transition for the new buyers. But sometimes, there are problems at the last minute that require assistance from the professionals.

In one transaction, the seller had moved out except for a few items of furniture. The buyer removed the items and left them for the seller to pick up. The buyer had moved into the house. The house now belongs to the buyer who holds title to it. The home no longer belongs to the seller. I emphasize this as the point of the story.

Yet, for some reason, the seller returned and decided he had the right to come into his former home once again. So, using a key he'd kept, the seller entered his old home without an invitation, and walked in on the buyers unannounced.

Fortunately, everyone was dressed and other than the shock of finding someone in their home, no one was shot and the police were not involved! Yet, the seller needed to be told in no uncertain terms that his rights had terminated. The new owners immediately changed all the locks!

Your real estate agent's job doesn't end when the escrow closes though. You have hopefully developed a close working relationship during the time you've worked together and forged some bonds that will survive the transaction. Questions arise and you'll want to call your agent for answers or advice.

A good agent will stay in touch with his clients. He'll keep them informed of the market conditions and issues that affect the value of their homes. The agent will be available to make referrals to professionals you may want to contact. It's always my goal to maintain a good relationship with my clients and see how they are doing in their new home. I want my clients to think of me when they make referrals to their friends and family. If I've done my job for them in the very best manner that I can, then I hope I'll have earned their trust. Thus, they will trust me with the sale or purchase of a home for someone they care about. A referral from a client is an honor that makes all the effort worthwhile!

We will have been on a significant, spiritual and intimate journey together. It is a privilege that my clients allow me to take that journey with them. My hope is that when all is finished, the journey will have been a good one and that every party will be satisfied that a good and fair deal has been done.

Good luck with all your transactions. May they all be successful and profitable!

www.ingramcontent.com/pod-product-compliance
Lightning Source LLC
Chambersburg PA
CBHW022023170526
45157CB00003B/1329